IN A PERSIAN MARKET.

Intermezzo-Scene.

ALBERT W. KETÈLBEY.

Synopsis.

The camel-drivers gradually approach the market; the cries of beggars for "Back-sheesh" are heard amid the bustle. The beautiful princess enters carried by her servants, (she is represented by a languorous theme, given at first to clarinet and cello, then repeated by full orchestra) — she stays to watch the jugglers and snake-charmer. The Caliph now passes through the market and interrupts the entertainment, the beggars are heard again, the princess prepares to depart and the caravan resumes its Journey; the themes of the princess and the camel-drivers are heard faintly in the distance and the market-place becomes deserted.

IN A PERSIAN MARKET.
Intermezzo Scene.

Arranged for Piano Duet
by the Composer.

SECONDO.

ALBERT W. KETÈLBEY.

"The camel-drivers gradually approach."
Andante con moto. (♩=108)

(*N. B.:— The Secondo player is to attend to the pedalling.*)

IN A PERSIAN MARKET.

Intermezzo Scene.

Arranged for Piano Duet
by the Composer.

PRIMO.

ALBERT W. KETÈLBEY.

"The camel-drivers gradually approach."

(N.B.:—The Primo player is to turn the pages.)

"The beggars in the market-place"

Bach-sheesh, back-sheesh, Al - lah,

Back-sheesh, back-sheesh, Al - lah, Back-sheesh, back-sheesh,

Al - - lah, Emp-shi! emp-shi! emp - - shi! *ff*

Poco meno mosso.

"The beggars in the market-place"

(*The top notes may be played by R.H. if prefered.*)

Poco meno mosso.

"The princess approaches."
melodia espressivo

"The princess approaches."

SECONDO.

Poco più mosso.

"The jugglers in the market-place."

Instead of semiquavers small notes may be played *ad lib.*

"The snake-charmer."

(like a drum)

(like Trumpets)

Poco più mosso.

"The jugglers in the market-place."

Brillante.

(Play small notes *ad lib.*)

"The snake-charmer."

loco

f Brillante.

Play small notes *ad lib.*

SECONDO.

"The Caliph passes."

ff *marziale marcato* (like Trumpets)

"The beggars are heard again."

dim.

mf

"The Princess departs."

p espressivo

Tempo I.
"The caravan resumes its journey."

Tempo I.
"The caravan resumes its journey"

"The princess in the distance."

"The princess in the distance".

(Secondo)

Sanctuary of the Heart

Méditation religieuse

Piano Duet

I wandered alone in a strange land,
And Life was so dark and drear,
When the sound of a voice seemed to call me
And brought to my mind a mem'ry dear;
It told of the Joy and the Gladness
That comes from the One above—
"O Lord, hear our pray'r,
Take away all our care,
And fill all our hearts with Love."

Arr. by the Composer

ALBERT W. KETÈLBEY

3230 (F)